W9-AEM-181

COOL SCIENCE

Experiments with Weather and Climate

By John Bassett

Gareth Stevens
Publishing

Please visit our Web site www.garethstevens.com. For a free color catalog of all our high-quality books, call toll free 1-800-542-2595 or fax 1-877-542-2596.

Library of Congress Cataloging-in-Publication Data
Bassett, John, 1978-
    Experiments with weather and climate / John Bassett.
        p. cm. -- (Cool science)
    Includes index.
    ISBN 978-1-4339-3447-6 (lib. bdg.) -- ISBN 978-1-4339-3448-3 (pbk.)
    ISBN 978-1-4339-3449-0 (6-pack)
    1. Weather--Experiments--Juvenile literature. 2. Climatology--Experiments--Juvenile literature.   I. Title.
QC981.3.B384 2010
551.6078--dc22   2009041575

Published in 2010 by
Gareth Stevens Publishing
111 East 14th Street, Suite 349
New York, NY 10003

© 2010 The Brown Reference Group Ltd.

For Gareth Stevens Publishing:
Art Direction: Haley Harasymiw
Editorial Direction: Kerri O'Donnell

For The Brown Reference Group Ltd:
Editorial Director: Lindsey Lowe
Managing Editor: Tim Harris
Editor: Sarah Eason
Children's Publisher: Anne O'Daly
Design Manager: David Poole
Designer: Paul Myerscough
Production Director: Alastair Gourlay

Picture Credits:
Front Cover: Corbis: Xinhau (foreground); Shutterstock: Victor Leonidovich Zastolskiy (background)
Title Page: Shutterstock: Victor Leonidovich Zastolskiy
iStock: Eric Hood 7, Parema 6b; NASA: 6t; Shutterstock: Photobank.kiev.ua 5, Rusian Nassyrov 4
All other images Martin Norris

Publisher's note to educators and parents: Our editors have carefully reviewed the Web sites that appear on p. 31 to ensure that they are suitable for students. Many Web sites change frequently, however, and we cannot guarantee that a site's future contents will continue to meet our high standards of quality and educational value. Be advised that students should be closely supervised whenever they access the Internet.

Manufactured in the United States of America
1 2 3 4 5 6 7 8 9   12 11 10

CPSIA compliance information: Batch #BRW0102GS: For further information contact Gareth Stevens, New York, New York at 1-800-542-2595.

Contents

Introduction

Weather forecasters rely on all sorts of amazing technology to predict the weather, such as satellites and radar images. But they also rely on the tried and tested instruments that have been around for many years. In the experiments in this book, you can build your own weather-detecting equipment to learn more about the weather.

Dark clouds gather in the sky. A thunderstorm is on the way.

The weather is an important part of our lives and affects everything that we do. In good weather, many people like relaxing in the sunshine. In the winter, people enjoy building snowmen and playing in the snow. It might be boring when you have to stay indoors to play on rainy days, but the rainwater is vital for growing crops that we need for our food. The weather can also destroy crops. Plants dry out and die when there is too much sunlight or a lack of water, for example, when the land freezes. Too much water can also damage crops, for example, during a flash flood. Every living thing, including humans, adapts to the weather in its environment. Sometimes animals, plants, and people cannot adapt quickly enough to survive if the weather changes dramatically.

What is the weather?

Several things play a part in forming the different types of weather around the world today. They include air temperature, air pressure, humidity (the amount of moisture in the air), and the wind speed and direction.

The Sun determines the temperature of the air. It shines most brightly around the equator. The Sun heats the land at the equator, and the hot air rises. As it does so it draws in cooler air from the north and south. In other parts of the world, cool air sinks. Air pressure is the weight of the air pushing down on Earth's surface. High air pressure is found in places where cool air is sinking. Low air pressure occurs in places where warm air is rising.

Wind is the movement of air from place to place. Wind carries heat away from the equator toward the polar regions. The wind also carries clouds. Life on Earth could not exist without the supply of freshwater from clouds. The water droplets in the clouds fall to the ground as rain, hail, sleet, and snow.

Palm trees bend in the direction of the prevailing wind.

LEARNING ABOUT SCIENCE

Doing experiments is the best way to learn about science. This is the way scientists test their ideas and find out new information. Follow this good science guide to get the most out of each experiment in this book.

• Never begin an experiment until you have talked to an adult about what you are going to do.
• Take care when you do or set up an experiment, whether it is dangerous or not. Make sure you know the safety rules before you start work. Wear goggles and use the right safety equipment when you are told to do so.
• Do each experiment more than once. The more times you carry out an experiment, the more accurate your results will be.
• Keep a notebook to record the results of your experiments. Make your results easy to read and understand. You can make notes and draw charts, diagrams, and tables.
• Drawing a graph is a great way of presenting your results. Plot the results of your experiment as dots on a graph. Use a ruler to draw a straight line through all the dots. Reading the graph will help you to fill in the gaps in your experiment.
• Write down the results as you do each experiment. If one result seems different from the rest, you might have made a mistake that you can fix immediately.
• Learn from your mistakes. Some of the most exciting findings in science came from an unexpected result. If your results do not tally with your predictions, try to find out why.

Bad weather

People often only notice the weather when it is bad. That is because bad weather can cause natural disasters such as blizzards, floods, hurricanes, and tornadoes. All of these extreme weather events can harm animals and plants and damage people's lives. Storms can devastate crops, destroy homes, and even kill people.

Predicting the weather

Since the weather changes so much, our ability to predict the weather accurately is very important. Scientists called meteorologists study Earth's atmosphere to predict the weather. Every day, meteorologists use a range of equipment to study clouds and the wind to see if they can predict when bad weather is on the way.

Hurricane Andrew

A wireless weather station records details such as air temperature and air pressure and sends the results to a computer for analysis.

This satellite image shows weather systems in Earth's atmosphere. The swirling mass of cloud is Hurricane Andrew. It hit the coast of Louisiana in August 1992, causing widespread devastation.

It is impossible to predict the weather with complete accuracy. Around the world, weather is constantly changing. Scientists cannot weigh up every possibility, but general patterns do occur. Meteorologists look out for these patterns to help them make their predictions. Some of the weather-detecting instruments that they use have been around for hundreds of years. The wind vane (to measure wind direction) and thermometer (to measure air temperature) have been around since the sixteenth century. The barometer (to measure air pressure) appeared around 100 years later. These early tools gave people the means to study the weather, and they are still used today.

CLIMATE CHANGE

Climate is the word that describes the average weather conditions of a particular place over a long period of time. Some people think that the climate is changing because of human activities such as cutting down forests and burning fossil fuels. Trees soak up carbon dioxide from the air and use it to make food from the Sun. If we cut down trees, there will be more carbon dioxide in the air. Burning fossil fuels also releases carbon dioxide into the air, as well as harmful gases such as nitrogen oxide and sulfur compounds.

All these gases are building up in Earth's atmosphere. They are trapping heat, which is warming the planet. As it warms, the ice frozen at the polar regions will start to melt, and sea levels will rise. Many cities around the world will become submerged if sea levels continue to rise at their current rate.

A meteorologist points out the center, or "eye," on this picture of a hurricane.

Modern meteorologists use satellites to take pictures of weather systems from space. Radar can show how much water is in clouds, so meteorologists can predict future rainfall. Balloons called radiosondes are sent high into the atmosphere to study the weather conditions. The data collected by all these different sources is fed into computers that try to model what the weather will be like. The information is then shown on weather maps so people can understand it.

Be a weather detective

Some of the activities in this book will help you become a real weather detective. You will have the chance to make equipment similar to the equipment used by real meteorologists. Then you can use it to measure the weather in your city or neighborhood. Weather forecasting relies on observation. Keep a notebook to record the weather conditions over several weeks. This will help you to predict the weather in the future.

BE SAFE!

One of the most important things to bear in mind when you are studying the weather is to realize how powerful and dangerous it can be. Never do any experiments in dangerous weather conditions such as floods, thunderstorms, or tornadoes. Flash floods can carry cars and trucks away in the water, and the force of a tornado can whisk whole houses into the air. Lightning strikes, though rare, can be deadly, too. The experiments in this book are all safe if you follow the instructions very carefully. If you are ever in any doubt about whether you should do an experiment because of the weather, ask an adult for help before you begin.

The Water Cycle

Goals

1 Make a working model of the water cycle.

2 Show how water evaporates, condenses, and then falls to Earth as rain.

LEVEL of Difficulty ✪ ✪ ✪
Hard   Medium   Easy

What you will need

- large plastic bowl
- small container
- water
- plastic wrap
- large rubber band
- two balls of modeling clay
- thermometer

1 Put the small container in the center of the large bowl. Hold it in place with a ball of modeling clay.

2 Fill the large bowl by pouring water around the edge of the small container. Make sure that no water spills into the small container.

3 Cover the two bowls with plastic wrap. Use a rubber band to secure it in place.

4 Put a ball of modeling clay in the center of the plastic wrap. The wrap should dip over the small container.

TROUBLESHOOTING

What if no water drips into the small container?

Some places are colder than others. You may need to repeat the activity with the bowl placed near a heater. If there is no sun, use a lightbulb or sunlamp. Once you have set up the experiment, do not move the bowl. Water could spill into the small bowl and your results may be misleading.

HOW A RAINDROP FORMS

Water moves between Earth and the atmosphere in a cycle called the water cycle. Raindrops form in clouds in Earth's lower atmosphere. As a cloud rises, it cools in the colder air. Some of the water vapor that makes up the cloud turns into tiny water droplets. The air in the clouds moves in currents that make the water droplets crash into each other. When they collide, the droplets join up. If enough of them cluster into a heavy drop, they fall back to Earth as rain. Sometimes raindrops form around tiny particles of dust, pollen, and salt.

SAFETY TIP!

If you leave the bowl under a lamp to warm the water, don't put it too close. You could melt the bowl and start a fire.

5 Leave the bowl setup in the Sun. See what happens to the water. Use a thermometer to take the temperature of the water in the small container.

A Hygrometer

What you will need

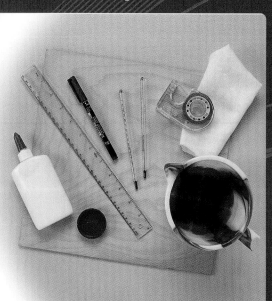

- chopping board
- ruler
- pen
- 2 thermometers
- glue
- bottle cap from a soda bottle
- muslin or cheesecloth
- water
- tape

Goals

1 Make a hygrometer.

2 Use it to measure the amount of humidity in the air.

LEVEL of Difficulty   ✦ Hard   ✦ Medium   ✦ Easy

2 Tape the two thermometers onto the board—side by side and level with each other. Leave a gap between them so that you can read them easily.

1 Draw evenly spaced lines on the board.

3 Glue the bottle cap about 1 inch (2.5cm) below one of the thermometers.

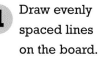

4 Prop up the board. Cut a small piece of muslin or cheesecloth. Dip it in water to wet it.

TROUBLESHOOTING

What if there is no difference in temperature between the two thermometers?

Make sure that the muslin is kept wet when you take each reading, otherwise you will only be taking the temperature and not finding the humidity. Also, make sure that the muslin stays in contact with the thermometer at all times.

5 Place the wet cloth in the bottle cap. Wrap the cloth around the bottom of the thermometer. Fill the cap with water. Wait about 30 minutes. Record the temperatures on the two thermometers. The lines on the board will help you to read them.

6 Leave the board outside. Wait 30 minutes and read the temperatures again. Is the difference in temperature higher or lower?

ADAPTING TO HUMIDITY

People keep cool by sweating. When sweat evaporates from our skin, it takes heat with it—helping to cool us down. In humid air, the sweat does not evaporate from our bodies to keep us cool. For this reason, running around in humid air can be exhausting if we are not used to it. It takes a while for our bodies to adapt to the humidity.

Making clouds

Goals

1 Show that clouds form from water vapor.

2 Recreate the way that clouds form.

What you will need

- jar
- hot water
- funnel
- ice cubes
- stopwatch or watch with second hans
- sheet of dark paper

1 Fill the jar with hot water from the faucet.

2 Place the funnel in the neck of the jar.

SAFETY TIP!

The water needs to be very hot for this activity to work. Make sure an adult is with you when you use hot water.

12

3 Fill the funnel with the ice cubes.

TROUBLESHOOTING

What if I can't see any clouds forming?

If you have trouble seeing the clouds forming, you may need to use hotter water. Ask an adult to pour boiling water into the jar. Do not touch the jar until the hot water has cooled down. Use oven mitts for safety.

DRY ICE

People make clouds and mist on stage, in movies, and in music videos using a process similar to this experiment. The difference is that they use frozen carbon dioxide, called dry ice, instead of ice cubes. Dry ice freezes at −110.2°F (−79°C)—cold enough to burn your hands. When dry ice mixes with boiling water in a dry ice machine, the carbon dioxide quickly changes back into a gas. The gas and water vapor is released through a hose at the front of the machine to make clouds.

4 Watch clouds of water vapor form over the funnel. Time how long it takes for the clouds to form. Place a sheet of dark paper behind the jar to make it easier to see the clouds.

Hailstones

What you will need

- 3 or 4 flexible containers of different sizes
- water
- freezer
- food dyes (at least 2 different colors)
- refrigerator
- cloth
- hammer
- tray
- measuring cup

Goals

1. Make your own hailstones.
2. Examine the different layers that form inside a hailstone.

LEVEL of Difficulty

Hard   Medium   Easy

SAFETY TIP!

Keep your free hand away from the hailstone when using the hammer.

 1 Pour water in the measuring cup. Add food dye for color. Pour the colored water into the smallest container. Put the container in the freezer.

2 Fill half of the next smallest container with water. Add a different food dye for color and mix well. Put this container in the fridge to chill. Make sure it does not freeze solid.

3 Remove the colored ice from the first container. Put a block of colored ice into the container of chilled water. Put it in the freezer and leave it to freeze.

4 Repeat steps 2 and 3 until you have used all the containers. Make sure you use a different color of food dye in each container. Alternate between two colors if that's all you have.

TROUBLESHOOTING

What if the hailstone doesn't freeze properly?

Chill the water before adding the hailstone to a new container. The ice will start to melt if you don't. Just tap the hailstone when you hit it with the hammer or you'll have no hailstone left!

5 Put the cloth on the tray. When the water in the last container is frozen solid, put your hailstone onto the cloth and cover it.

GIANT HAILSTONES

The largest hailstone reported in the United States fell in Coffeyville, Kansas, in September 1970. The hailstone measured 17.5 inches (44.5cm) across and weighed 1⅔ pounds (0.7kg).

6 Gently tap the hailstone with a hammer to break it open and reveal the layers inside.

Making a Flood

Goals

1 Make a model to show how floodplains flood.

2 Use rocks and sponges to show what type of ground is most likely to flood.

LEVEL of Difficulty Hard Medium **Easy**

What you will need

- large bowl
- large tray
- sponges
- measuring cup
- water
- watering can
- freezer
- rocks

1 Put the bowl in the center of the tray. Put pieces of dry sponge around the edge of the bowl.

2 Pour water into the bowl.

SAFETY TIP!

Take care when carrying heavy rocks. Use both hands to carry them.

3 Fill the watering can with water. Record the amount of water you put into the can. Then pour water onto the bowl and the sponges. This is the rain.

4 Keep pouring water over your model until the bowl starts to overflow and you can see water on top of the sponges. You might need to refill the watering can. Record the total amount of water it takes to flood the tray.

TROUBLESHOOTING

What if the water overflows onto the floor?

This activity can get messy. It is best to do it somewhere, such as the back yard, where it doesn't matter if the floor gets wet. Put the wet sponges on a tray in the freezer to make sure they don't stick to the freezer itself. If you want to see the effects of a heavy rainstorm, use a hose instead of the watering can. Make sure an adult is with you when you use the hose.

5 Put the wet sponges on a tray in the freezer. Take them out when they are frozen. Repeat the activity. How much water does it take to flood the tray when the sponges are frozen?

6 Repeat the activity using rocks instead of sponges. How much water does it take to flood the tray now?

Rainbows

What you will need

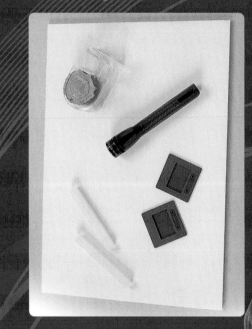

- flashlight with a narrow beam
- 4 to 6 glue sticks
- white cloth, paper, or wall as a background
- clear sticky tape
- 2 polarizing filters
- assistant

Goals

1 Find out how the atmosphere scatters light to make blue sky and red sunsets.

2 See why the sky is sometimes different colors at different times of the day.

LEVEL of Difficulty   ✦ Hard   ✦ Medium   ✦ Easy

2 Put two glue sticks end to end. Join them up with clear sticky tape.

1 Shine the flashlight into one end of the glue stick. Hold the other end of the glue stick about ½ inch (1cm) from the white background. The end of the glue stick closest to the flashlight is a different color from the end closest to the white background. Note the color of the circle on the white background.

3 Repeat step 1. Note any differences in the colors along the glue sticks and in the colored circle on the background. Tape more glue sticks together and repeat step 1. How do the colors change as you add more glue sticks?

TROUBLESHOOTING

I didn't notice any color changes.

This activity works best if you use a narrow-beam flashlight. If you cannot find a narrow-beam flashlight, turn off all the lights to make the flashlight's beam brighter.

4 Have an assistant hold two polarizing filters up to his or her eyes. Point a glue stick at your partner. Shine the flashlight through it. Ask your friend to rotate the filters. What does he or she see?

SAFETY TIP !

Never shine a flashlight directly into someone's eyes. The light is bright and can damage the eyes or blind someone.

REMEMBER THE RAINBOW

There are many different ways to help you remember the order of the colors in a rainbow. One of them is the name ROY G. BIV (first letters of red, orange, yellow, green, blue, indigo, and violet).

5 If you only have one polarizing filter, hold it between the glue stick and the flashlight. Rotate it and look at the filter from the side.

A Weather Vane

Goals

1 Make a weather vane.

2 Use your weather vane to show wind direction.

LEVEL of Difficulty

Hard Medium Easy

What you will need

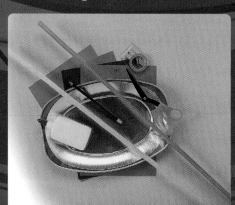

- strip of balsa wood 4 feet (1.2m) long
- wooden dowel 3 foot (0.9m) long
- aluminum tray
- tack
- metal washer

- white glue
- colored card

- scissors and pencil
- compass

1 Use scissors to cut a piece of balsa wood about 2 feet (60cm) long.

2 Use a pencil to mark an arrow head and a tail shape on the aluminum tray. Make sure that they are big enough to catch the wind. Cut out the shapes.

SAFETY TiP !

Take care when you use scissors and tacks. An adult should be with you when you use any tools or sharp objects.

3 Cut a small, vertical slit in each end of the piece of balsa wood. The slits need be about ½ inch (1cm) deep. Put some glue on one slit, and push the arrow head into the slit. Repeat with the tail. Put the structure to one side to dry for at least an hour.

4 Put the washer on the end of the long wooden dowel. Push a tack through the midpoint of the balsa wood, through the washer, and into the wooden dowel. Turn the balsa wood around several times to make sure that it spins freely.

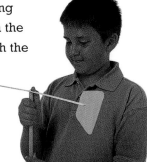

5 Draw an outline of the letters N (north), S (south), E (east), and W (west) onto colored card. Use a different color for each letter. Cut out the letters.

7 Take your weather vane outside. Use a compass to find north. Push your weather vane into the ground, with the "N" facing north. The arrow head will point in the direction the wind is blowing from. Note the wind direction every day.

6 Cut four pieces of balsa wood, each 6 inches (15cm) long. Glue a letter to each strip of balsa wood. Glue the wood strips onto the dowel. Make sure you leave your weather vane to dry for at least an hour.

An Anemometer

What you will need

- old newspaper
- 4 Styrofoam cups
- paint
- paintbrush
- scissors
- wooden strip about 18 inches (45cm) long
- wooden dowel about 3 feet (0.9m) long
- pencil
- 5 thumbtacks
- washer
- stopwatch
- ruler

Goals

1. Build an anemometer.
2. Use it to measure wind speed.

LEVEL of Difficulty — Hard   Medium   Easy

1 Put newspaper on your work surface to protect it. Paint the outside of one of the Styrofoam cups.

2 Cut the wooden strip in half. Use a pencil to mark the midpoint of each piece of wood with an "X." Put the two Xs over each other. Push a tack through both pieces of wood.

3 Pin the cups to the ends of the wooden strips. Make sure all the cups face in the same direction.

SAFETY TIP !
Always cut away from your body when you are using scissors.

4 Put a washer on top of the wooden dowel. Push the tack in the wooden strip through the washer and into the top of the dowel. The washer will act as a spacer so the cups can revolve.

5 Take your anemometer outside to measure the wind speed. Push the wooden dowel into the dirt or tie it to a fence. Make sure the cups can spin freely.

TROUBLESHOOTING

What if the cups do not revolve?

Test your anemometer before you use it. Blow on the cups to make sure that they spin. You might need to pull the thumbtack out slightly. Make sure that each arm of the anemometer is exactly the same length. If not, your anemometer will be inaccurate.

STRONG WIND

The highest recorded wind speed over land was 231 miles per hour (372km/h) at Mount Washington, New Hampshire, on April 12, 1934. The windiest place on Earth is Commonwealth Bay, George V Coast, Antarctica, where wind speeds sometimes reach 199 miles per hour (320km/h).

6 Measure the wind speed by counting the number of times the colored cup revolves in one minute. (It is easier with two people—one person timing and one counting.) This will tell you the wind speed in revolutions (turns) per minute.

Build a Barometer

Goals

1 Make a barometer to measure air pressure.

2 Predict the weather from changes in pressure.

LEVEL of Difficulty

⬡ Hard ⬢ Medium ⬡ Easy

What you will need

- posterboard
- scissors
- pen
- ruler
- plastic plate
- tape
- balloon
- glass
- straw
- glue/double-sided tape

1 Cut a strip of posterboard 3 inches (7.5cm) wide and about 8 inches (20cm) long.

2 Use a ruler and pen to mark lines on the posterboard every ¼ inch (6mm). Start 3 inches (7.5cm) from the bottom. Number each line.

3 Bend the strip 1 inch (2.5cm) from the bottom to make a flap. Cut a slit in the flap. Tape the strip onto the plate so that it stands up.

4 Cut the narrow end off the balloon.

 5 Stretch the balloon over the glass so that the top of the glass is covered and the balloon is tight.

6 Cut the straw to make a point at one end. Dab glue on the blunt end of the straw. Lay it on the balloon. Make sure 5 inches (12.5cm) of the straw hang over the side of the glass.

7 Put the glass on the plate so the pointed end of the straw overlaps the card. Look at your barometer several times each day. Record the position of the straw and the time of day in your notebook. Also note what the weather is like.

TROUBLESHOOTING

What if the straw does not move?

Depending on the time of year, the air pressure may remain stable for long periods. So it might be that the air pressure has not changed much. Make sure the balloon is stretched tightly across the top of the glass. Try to keep the barometer out of direct sunlight because it will heat the air inside. This will make the air expand and give false readings.

Making a Thermometer

What you will need

- water and ice
- rubbing alcohol
- clear, narrow-necked glass bottle or jar
- funnel
- measuring cup
- food coloring
- clear plastic drinking straw
- modeling clay
- white paper and tape
- pen and scissors

Goals

1 See how liquids expand and contract as they get warmer and cooler.

2 Make a thermometer and use it to record the temperature.

LEVEL of Difficulty — Hard · Medium · Easy

1 Use a funnel to pour equal amounts of cold alcohol and water into the bottle or jar. Fill it to the top.

2 Add a few drops of food coloring to the bottle. Swirl it around to mix the liquids.

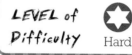

3 Ask an adult to punch a hole in the lid of the bottle or jar. Put the straw through the hole so that it dips into the liquid. Seal it with modeling clay so the straw stays in place.

SAFETY TiP !

Rubbing alcohol is safe to touch, but it can be dangerous to drink it. Breathing in the fumes can make you dizzy. Keep the alcohol away from your mouth, eyes, and nose at all times.

4 Cut out a strip of paper. Tape it to the straw.

5 The liquid will rise up the straw as it warms up to room temperature. Label the level it reaches on the paper "Room Temperature."

TROUBLESHOOTING

What if the liquid doesn't rise very far up the straw?

The alcohol and water mixture should be very cold to begin with so it expands a lot when it warms up to room temperature. If water from the faucet isn't cold enough, mix the alcohol and water and store it in the fridge before you start the activity. Adding a little extra liquid through the straw after you have sealed the bottle will help, too.

HIGH TEMPERATURES

Liquid-in-glass thermometers cannot be used to measure very hot temperatures because they can break or melt. Mercury thermometers are used up to the boiling point of mercury—674°F (357°C). An instrument called an optical pyrometer is used to measure very high temperatures, such as those inside stars. It compares the color of the starlight to the color of light given off by a lamp at a known temperature.

6 Put the thermometer in a beaker of warm water. When the liquid stops rising, mark the level on the paper. Label it "Warm Water."

7 Put your thermometer in a beaker of icy water. Leave it for a few minutes. Mark the level on the paper. Label it "Cold Water."

Energy from the Sun

Goals

1 Find the best way to soak up heat from the Sun.

LEVEL of Difficulty — Hard — Medium — Easy

What you will need

- 2 plastic bottles
- 2 balloons
- 2 rubber bands
- black poster paint
- white poster paint
- newspaper
- lamp or sunny day
- paintbrushes

1 Paint one of the plastic bottles white. Paint the other bottle black.

2 Put a balloon over the neck of each bottle. Hold the balloons in place using rubber bands.

HANDY HINTS

Cover the work surface with newspaper before painting the bottles. Secure the balloons tightly to the bottles because you do not want air to leak out.

TROUBLESHOOTING

What *if nothing happens* to the balloons?

If it is cool, you may not notice any changes in your balloons. Put the bottles where there is the most sunlight. Check that the balloons are tightly secured to the bottles. If there are any holes or leaks in the balloons, you will not see any changes.

3 Leave both bottles in the sunshine. What happens to the balloons?

4 You should see one of the balloons stand upright as the air inside the bottle expands. When this happens, move both bottles into the shade. What happens now?

5 You can still do the activity if there is no sunshine, using a lamp to warm the bottles instead. Position the lamp so that it shines directly on the balloons, about 6 inches (15cm) above them.

SAFETY TIP!

If you use a lamp, don't put it too close to the balloons. The heat could melt the balloons or the plastic bottles.

Glossary

anemometer: device for measuring wind speed

atmosphere: layer of gas that surrounds a planet

barometer: a device used to measure air pressure

blizzard: heavy snowfall in very windy conditions

climate: the average weather conditions of a particular place over a long period of time

compass: a instrument used to find magnetic north, helping people find their way

condense: to turn from a gas (such as water vapor) into a liquid

dry ice: the frozen form of carbon dioxide

equator: an imaginary line that forms a circle around Earth, halfway between the North Pole and the South Pole

evaporate: to turn from a liquid to a gas

flash flood: a sudden flood caused by heavy rain falling on hard, dry ground

floodplains: flat area of ground around a river over which the river sometimes floods

humidity: the amount of water vapor in the air

hurricane: a tropical storm over the Atlantic Ocean that features extremely strong winds

hygrometer: device for measuring humidity

lightning: a powerful discharge of electricity during a storm

meteorologist: a scientist who studies the weather and tries to predict future weather events

optical pyrometer: device that measures the temperature of an object by the radiation it gives off

radar: short for radio detection and ranging, radar finds objects, such as clouds, by bouncing radio waves off them

satellite: an object that spins around Earth. Meteorologists use satellites to help predict the weather.

Styrofoam: a very light plastic filled with air bubbles

temperature: a measure of the heat in something

thermometer: an instrument used to measure temperature

thunder: the noise of the shock wave made when lightning strikes

tornado: a high-speed, swirling current of air that sometimes forms during thunderstorms

wind: the movement of air from an area of high pressure to an area of low pressure

wind vane: device for measuring wind direction

vapor: another word meaning "gas." For example, water vapor is steam.

Further Information

BOOKS

Cosgrove, Brian. *Weather*. New York: Dorling Kindersley, 2007.

Orr, Tamara. *Super Cool Science Experiments: Weather*. North Mankato, MN: Cherry Lake Publishing, 2009.

Rubin, Joel. *Science Fair Projects: Weather*. Mankato MN: Heinemann Educational Books, 2007.

Tocci, Salvatore. *Experiments with Air*. New York: Children's Press, 2003.

Williams, Zella. *Experiments on the Weather*. New York: PowerKids Press, 2007.

WEBSITES

www.its.caltech.edu/~atomic/snowcrystals/

www.wxdude.com

www.weatherwizkids.com

Index